The L_____ of

Dinosaurs

for Kids of All Ages

Zymurgy Publishing

Zymurgy Publishing
The moral rights of author
Martin Ellis/Zymurgy
Publishing have been asserted.

Image credits: Paul Goldsmith, Deposit Photos -Digital Studio, Pixel Chaos, Corey Ford, Vaeenma, Nelid, Rex Wisconsin Art, Dreamstime Fabio Lozzino, Nickolai Shitov, Kitti Kahotong, Andrej Antic, Derrick Neill, Adrianadh, Andreas Meyer, Linda Bucklin.

A CIP catalogue record for this book is available from the British library.
Printed & bound by
ISBN 978 1903506 509
Published by Zymurgy Publishing
Newcastle upon Tyne
10 9 8 7 6 5 4 3 2 1
© Zymurgy Publishing 2022

Contents

Triassic Period

250 mill. to 200 mill..years ago

Jurassic Period

200 mill..years to 145 mill years ago

Cretaceous Period

145 mill.to 65 mill. years ago

Cenozoic Era

65 mill. years ago until now

Triassic, Jurassic and Cretaceous periods
are the 3 different dinosaurs eras.

Introduction

Dinosaurs ruled the Earth for millions of years, millions of years ago. We are learning a lot about dinosaurs. In fact more has been learned about dinosaurs in the last 20 years than in the previous 200 years!

200 years ago, when people wanted to learn about dinosaurs, they looked at dinosaur fossils. Fossils are still very important to people studying dinosaurs. However, with modern scientific technology it is possible to learn much more from fossils.

Almost every week a new dinosaur species is found. That's nearly 50 new dinosaurs a year.

In this book there are answers to many questions about dinosaurs. As you get older, scientists will discover new dinosaurs, and we will learn more about dinosaurs.

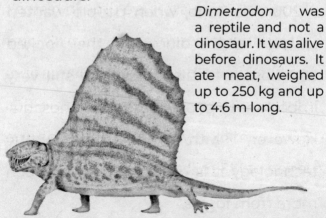

Dimetrodon was a reptile and not a dinosaur. It was alive before dinosaurs. It ate meat, weighed up to 250 kg and up to 4.6 m long.

What Is A Dinosaur?

Dinosaurs were reptiles that lived millions of years ago, so long ago that they are prehistoric. A time so long ago that it could be called before history – although, obviously, it is a time in history.

It is difficult to be exact about how long ago the first dinosaurs lived. Dinosaurs lived in a time called the Mesozoic Era: 250 - 65 million years ago. That's a time period of 185 million years!

Humans and Reptiles

Scientists can't agree on how long humans like ourselves have lived on Earth, but they all agree it is a short time compared to dinosaurs.

Reptiles are mainly cold-blooded animals that breathe air and lay eggs. Reptiles that exist today include lizards, crocodiles, alligators, snakes and turtles. Reptiles have backbones, are covered with scales and have at least one lung.

What was the land on Earth like before the first dinosaurs?

At the start of the Mesozoic Period, instead of 7 continents, the planet Earth had one huge area of land surrounded by sea. The land was called Pangaea and the sea that surrounded the land was called Panthalassa. Pangaea covered about a third of the Earth's surface, which is similar to the amount of land on Earth today. Most of Pangaea was in the south of the Earth.

Pangaea

The word 'Pangaea' comes from Greek words, 'pan' and 'gaia' meaning 'all Earth'.

Animals from the time of dinosaurs that are still around today

There are animals around today that lived at the same time as dinosaurs. Sadly, some of these animals are now in danger of extinction after surviving millions of years.

Crocodilian is the name of the group of animals that includes crocodiles, alligators, caimans and gharials. Crocodiles have lived on Earth for about 240 million years.

Snake fossils prove that snakes have

been around since 140 to 167 million years ago. So they were not around at the start of the dinosaur period, but from around the middle of the time of dinosaurs.

Sharks were swimming around the oceans before the first dinosaurs. The first sharks date back 450 million years. Sharks have survived 4 mass extinction events - that's times when almost all life on Earth has been killed!

Sharks used to eat dinosaurs. *Spinosaurus* dinosaurs used to eat sharks. The *Spinosuarus* is the largest known meat-eating dinosaur. It was larger than the *Tyrannosaurus*: its body was between 14 and 18 metres long and it weighed between 13 and 22 tonnes. Its skull was 1.75 metres long. As well as sharks, they used to eat fish. How do we know? Spinosaurus fossils have been found with fish bones in their stomachs.

Horseshoe Crabs are sometimes called 'living fossils'. They evolve or change very slowly, so modern day Horseshoe Crabs are very similar to Horseshoe Crabs living in the time of dinosaurs.

During the time of dinosaurs there were many **insect and bee** species. Some are now extinct, some are still around. However, many insects during the time of dinosaurs are now extinct.

Prehistoric insects were much bigger than today's insects. Perhaps this was because there was much more oxygen in the air, or it might have been because the Earth was warmer and moister. Nobody really knows, but we do know that insect fossils prove that in the time of dinosaurs there were giant insects. Insects have also been found trapped in amber, which is fossilised tree resin.

The **Duck-billed Platypus** is an egg-laying mammal (monotreme) which is still around today. They live in wet parts of Australia and Tasmania. They like swimming and also live on land. Sadly, they are now an animal at risk of extinction.

Green Sea Turtles are one of the largest sea turtles. They are unusual because they are carnivores when they are young (eat meat) but when they are fully grown, they are herbivores (they eat plants). A major problem for sea turtles is that they eat plastic bags, which can lead to their death. Green Sea Turtles are now at risk after surviving for millions of years, due to plastic in our seas and the destruction of where they live and what they eat.

Earth during the Triassic Period, Pangea starting to break-up

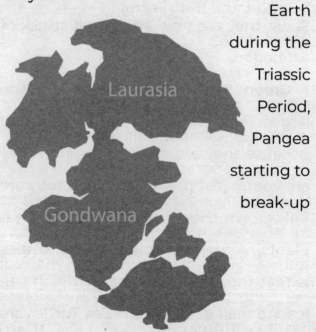

Laurasia

Gondwana

Before Dinosaurs

The time before dinosaurs is the Permian Period

Throughout the Permian Period the Earth got hotter.

There were animals on Earth before dinosaurs; many were killed off before the first dinosaurs. During this time there were bony fish, sharks and amphibians (animals that live partly in water and partly on land. Modern day amphibians include frogs, toads, salamanders and newts). Synapsids were mammal-like reptiles with skeletons similar to early reptiles.

Plants in the Permian Period were mainly shrubs, ferns and conifers. The Earth was very, very hot. It might have been as hot as 74 degrees C at the equator. The Permian Period ended with an event sometimes called the 'the Great Dying' because almost all plant and animal life was killed.

In Montana in America, the 330-million-year-old fossil of an octopus was found. It existed millions of years before the first dinosaurs. It is different to a modern octopus, with 10 limbs instead of 8. The fossil has been named *Syllipsimopodi*

Bideni after American President Joe Biden.

Before dinosaurs there were reptiles and insects. Some of them were huge. For example, *Meganeura* were like giant dragonflies, 40 cm long with a wingspan of 70cm. '*Meganeura*' means 'large-nerved' and the insects were called this because they had a large network of veins in their big wings. A large reptile that looks similar to a dinosaur is the *Dimetrodon*. The *Dimetrodon* had a large sail on its back, which it probably used to 'catch the sun' so it could warm up.

The Mesozoic Era

Consists of triassic, jurassic and cretaceous periods.

The Triassic Period started just over 250 million years ago and ended just over 200 million years ago. It lasted for about 50 million years.

It started after 'The Great Dying' a time of mass extinction with almost every animal on Earth dying - 9 out of 10 animals died. It was much more severe than the event that killed off dinosaurs millions of years later.

The first dinosaurs appeared in the

middle of the Triassic period, between 240 and 230 million years ago.

The first dinosaurs were small; some were the size of a modern pet cat. They walked on 2 legs. Their legs went straight down from their bodies, which was different to many reptiles that had legs at the side of their body (a good example is a crocodile).

The first dinosaurs were better at hunting and finding food than other animals, so over millions of years, they evolved and became larger than other animals.

Earth during the Jurassic Period, Laurasia
and Godwana starting to break-up

The Jurassic Period

The Jurassic Period was the middle period for dinosaurs, starting nearly 200 million years ago and ending about 145 million years ago. The climate changed from being dry to becoming wet, and warm instead of hot. The climate change helped plants to grow, and there were lots of trees and shrubs similar to palm trees called cycads. There were so many cycads that the Jurassic era is sometimes called 'the Age of Cycads'. There were also many conifer forests and ferns growing.

At the start of the Jurassic Period, Pangaea (the large single land mass) started to break up into 2 super-continents. They were called Laurasia and Gondwana and there were oceans to the east and west of them. When the land masses started to break up, the climate started to get warmer and wetter and lakes and swamp land were created. The swamps and lakes were key to dinosaur fossils forming to be discovered millions of years later.

The Jurassic period was also the time when big dinosaurs first arrived on Earth. Mammals were small and dinosaurs dominated the planet.

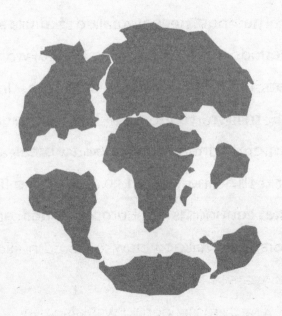

Earth during the Cretaceous Period

The Cretaceous Period

The most recent of the 3 dinosaur periods is the Cretaceous Period, which ran from 145 million years ago until 65 million years ago. The Pangaean supercontinent continued to break up and the land started to look more like the continents of Europe, Africa and Asia that we know now.

What is a fossil?

Fossils provide most of the information we have about dinosaurs. So, what is a fossil?

Fossils are the remains of animals, insects or plants that have been preserved in rock.

Fossils can be made in different ways, but most fossils are made when an animal dies in watery mud, and is then covered up by more mud. Then, over millions of years more and more mud covers the animal's remains and as the weight of mud gets heavier, it compacts (or gets pressed together) to become rock.

There are two main types of fossil. Body fossils are when the fossil is made from the remains of the animal or plant. Trace fossils are fossils that preserve footprints and animal tracks.

The study of fossils is called *paleontology* and a person who studies fossils is called a *paleontologist*. The word fossil comes from a Latin word, '*fossillis*' which means 'got by digging'.

Not all fossils are discovered by digging!

When the sea washes away cliffs, people have sometimes discovered fossils.

Lily Wilder, a four-year-old girl walking along Bendricks beach in South Wales in 2021, discovered a dinosaur footprint which had just been uncovered.

Also in 2021, 10-metre *Ichthyosaur* fossil was uncovered when a lake was drained in Rutland. It was not a dinosaur, but it lived at the same time as dinosaurs.

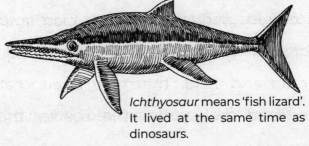

Ichthyosaur means 'fish lizard'. It lived at the same time as dinosaurs.

Why do some places have many fossils?

Some places, like the Jurassic Coast where Mary Anning lived, contain many more fossils than others. For dead animals to become fossils, the ground and conditions need to be right. In the time of dinosaurs, wet marshland would be ideal for forming fossils. A dead animal falling on this type of ground would be covered gradually by layer upon layer of sediment. Sediment is grains of rock, mud and sand. The more layers that covered the animal, the heavier the layers would become and they would press together over millions of years to become hard rock. After about 10,000 years, the bones and teeth of the dead dinosaur would become fossilised rock. The type of rock made by layer after layer of sediment is called sedimentary rock, so more fossils are found in places that have sedimentary rock.

In forests and jungles dead animals on the ground are eaten by other animals. So there were probably many species of dinosaurs that lived in forests and jungles which didn't become fossils.

Who invented the word dinosaur?

Before 1847 nobody talked about dinosaurs, because the word hadn't been created. People did talk about prehistoric animals and monsters.

Sir Richard Owen was born in Lancashire in 1804. Apparently he was from a poor background and at school was described as 'impudent' (cheeky). He helped set up the Natural History museum in London.

After noticing that fossil remains had similar distinctive features, he called them 'terrible lizards' and thought that the family of animals needed a name. The word 'dinosaur' is based on two Greek words: '*deinos*' which means 'awesome', or 'terrible', and '*sauros*' which is the Greek word for 'lizard'. In English, the word became 'dinosaur'.

Sir Richard Owen started his working life as a medical doctor, then he became a scientist and studied animal bones. London Zoo gave him the right to be the first person to be asked if they wished to have a dead animal to study. One day his wife came home and found a dead rhinoceros on her doorstep.

Plateosaurus means 'flat lizard' or 'broad lizard'. A plant eating dinosaur from the the Triassic Period. Bipedal - it walked on 2 legs, it could grow to be up to 8 metres long. It was one of the first large dinosaurs and could run at speeds of up to 40 mph.

How are dinosaurs named?

Dinosaur names are usually a combination of two words in Greek or Latin.

The first part of the name usually links to the general family of dinosaurs that the dinosaur belongs to.

The second part of the name is unique to the particular species of dinosaur.

So, how does a dinosaur get a unique name? Well, it may be due to something unusual about the dinosaur, such as big feet, or a long head. Sometimes it may be related to the place that the dinosaur was found. Sometimes, but not very often, it is the name of the person who discovered the dinosaur.

All dinosaur names now need to be approved by the International Commission on Zoological Nomenclature. Once they have checked that the dinosaur hasn't already been discovered and given a name, or the name hasn't been given to another dinosaur, the name is made official.

Other languages have been used to

name dinosaurs. For example the *Changuraptor* from north east China uses the Chinese word for 'long feather' which is '*changu*' and 'raptor' is a word used for animals that grab and take other animals to eat. The word '*raptor*' is usually used to describe birds that kill and eat other animals.

Main types of Dinosaur

Dinosaurs can be grouped together using different methods

Dividing Dinosaurs into 3 groups

Some people like to divide dinosaurs into 3 groups; meat-eaters (carnivores), plant-eaters (herbivores) and dinosaurs that eat both meat and plants (omnivores).

Dividing Dinosaurs into 2 groups

Dinosaurs can be divided into 2 different types based on their pelvis (the part of the body that contains the hips and thighs). The 2 different pelvis types are bird-hipped pelvises, which are *Ornithischian* dinosaurs, and lizard-hipped, which are *Saurischian* dinosaurs.

Dividing Dinosaurs into subgroups based on their characteristics

Saurischian dinosaurs can be divided into 2 groups

Theropods - this word means 'beast-footed'. *Therapods* had 3 toes with claws on each limb. They were bipedal, which means they walked on 2 legs. Almost all *Theropods* ate meat. They were similar in some ways to birds. For example, they had feathers, bones filled with air and they used to brood over their eggs. The *Tyrannosaurus Rex* was a *Therapod*.

Sauropodmorphs were long-necked, long-tailed plant-eaters and include some of the largest dinosaurs ever - the *sauropods*. Their necks were longer than their bodies and often longer than their limbs. They had small heads and solid, heavy bones. They were not very fast and probably would amble along on all 4 legs a bit like elephants.

One of the tallest dinosaurs ever discovered was a sauropod: *Barosaurus* was 22 metres tall – about the height of 4 tall giraffes. The *Diplodocus* was also a *Sauropod*.

Ornithischian can be divided into 3 groups

Marginocephalians this word means 'fringed heads'. Within this group, the *Pachycephalosauria* had a thick bone on the top of their skulls, which they used to head-butt predators, and the *Ceratopsia* had horns on their heads to help defend themselves. *Marginocephalians* were herbivores. The *Triceratops* was a type of *Marginocephalian*.

Ornithorpods - the name comes from Latin: '*ornitho*' means 'bird' and '*pod*' means 'foot' so their name means 'bird foot'. They ate plants. The first *ornithorpods* were quite small, less than a metre long, but over time they evolved to become much larger. They would run on 2 legs but when grazing, often in groups or herds, they would be on 4 legs. The Iguanodon was a type of *Ornithorpod*.

Thyreophorans this word means 'shield bearers'. *Thyreophorans* were armoured dinosaurs that were mainly plant-eaters. Some were quite small, about a metre long, and could run quite quickly. Others were much bigger and moved more slowly. The most famous sub-group of *Thyreophorans* are the *Stegosaurus*.

The *Stegosaurus* was a huge dinosaur with a small brain. Its brain was about the same size as a dog's brain. Compared to many dinosaurs, it moved quite slowly with a maximum

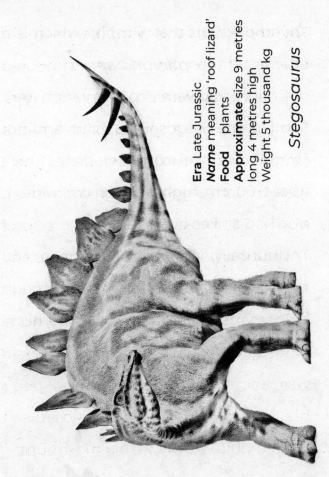

Era Late Jurassic
Name meaning 'roof lizard'
Food plants
Approximate size 9 metres
long 4 metres high
Weight 5 thousand kg

Stegosaurus

45

speed estimated at 5 mph, which is a little faster than people can walk.

On its back were 17 plates which were fixed to the Stegosaurus's skin and not fixed to its skeleton. The plates were about 60 cm high and 60 cm wide. It also had spikes on its tail.

Unusually, it ate small stones and rocks which helped to mash up tough plant matter such as ferns in its stomach.

Could dinosaurs fly?

None of the dinosaurs that lived in the Triassic, Jurassic or Cretaceous Periods could fly.

The main flying animals that were related to dinosaurs are *Pterosaurs*. Many people mistake *Pterosaurs* for dinosaurs. However, they are not dinosaurs; they are reptiles.

The name *Pterosaur* means 'winged lizard'. Their wings were made of skin instead of feathers. You could think of *Pterosaurs* as dinosaur cousins and they lived at the same time as dinosaurs.

Apart from insects, they were the first animals to fly. They were not birds, but were similar to birds in some ways. For example, their bones were hollow and filled with air.

Their wings stretched out from a fourth finger of their arm. The smallest pterosaur had a wingspan of about 25 cm and the largest had a huge wingspan of just over 10 metres!

However, did you know that scientists consider modern birds to be dinosaurs - and birds can fly!

Pterosaur

Are birds dinosaurs?

Scientists agree that birds are a type of dinosaur. Birds are part of the *Theropod* group of dinosaurs. So, birds are related to one of the greatest dinosaurs ever, the *T. Rex*. *Theropods* are all bipedal, which means they walk on 2 legs - just like birds.

Another dinosaur that looks even more like a bird is a *Velociraptor*. 'Vello' means 'swift' or 'very fast' and 'raptor' means 'robber' or 'grab'. So, *Velociraptor* got its name from being a fast-moving thief.

No dinosaurs were able to fly in prehistoric times, although some of them may have been able to glide. They might have been able to jump from trees or perhaps jump from other places where they would perch. Nobody really knows.

Velociraptor

Could dinosaurs swim?

Some people say dinosaurs couldn't swim. Many dinosaur experts argue that they could. After all, elephants, horses, dogs and obviously humans can swim. Perhaps a better question is 'were dinosaurs good at swimming'? The answer is probably that dinosaurs were not great swimmers.

So, did dinosaurs live in water? No, they were animals that lived on land, some dinosaurs were able to enter water to hunt for food.

Baryonyx walkeri was discovered in

1983 in a clay pit in Surrey, in England. '*Baryonyx*' means 'heavy claw' and it was called '*walkeri*' is because it was discovered by a Mr Walker. This dinosaur was a *Theropod* (a type of dinosaur that is carnivorous and walks on 2 legs) and it lived 125 - 160 million years ago. Scientists found fish scales in its stomach, which proved that some land-based dinosaurs also spent time in water.

Spinosaurus: a dinosaur that swam

However, there is a dinosaur that was a good swimmer: the *Spinosaurus*. It was a therapod that lived on land and water in what is now north Africa. It was a member of the *Spinosauridae* family of dinosaurs.

Why do we think that *Spinosaurus* could swim? It had webbed feet and a long flexible tail which would help propel it along when in it was in the water. Its nostrils were near the top of its snout so it would have been easier to breathe when it was swimming. It usually walked on two legs, but it could walk on all fours as well. It might have been able to run as fast as 15 miles an hour.

The *Spinosaurus* is the largest dinosaur. It was bigger than a *T Rex*. Its skull was as big as a man (182 cm), while a *T. Rex* skull was only the size of a small child. The head and jaw look similar to modern crocodiles. It had a line of sharp, straight teeth like knives, unlike most meat-eating dinosaurs, which had curved teeth.

The *Spinosaurus* lived 30 million years before the *T.Rex* so they would not have been able to fight each other. They are in a fight in the film Jurassic Park III but this would have been impossible.

It ate meat and fish. It would have eaten sharks, fish and other dinosaurs - in fact anything it wanted. Its sharp claws would capture prey and its teeth would cut through flesh and bones.

Spinosaurus's most distinctive feature was the large sail of long spines covered in skin along its back. This sail was more than 2 metres high.

Spinosaurus

Were dinosaurs warm or cold blooded?

Although most reptiles are cold-blooded, and many dinosaurs would have been cold-blooded, some dinosaurs may have been warm-blooded. Dinosaurs were probably 'mesotherms' and were able to control their body temperature. At some point of dinosaur development, dinosaurs would have become warm blooded.

Modern reptiles are not related to dinosaurs.

Cold-blooded animals (*ectotherms*), like reptiles, can't control their own body temperature. They have to get heat from their environment (that's why lizards bask in the sun). Cold-blooded animals move more slowly and grow more slowly.

Warm-blooded animals (*endotherms*), like mammals and birds, generate their own heat

What was dinosaur skin like?

What colour were dinosaurs?

Some dinosaurs would have had very little colouring; other dinosaurs were covered in feathers, which could have been brightly coloured and the feathers may have had a pattern. It is thought that some dinosaurs had brightly coloured heads. It is thought that smaller dinosaurs would have had less colourful skins, so that they would be less likely to be seen by meat-eating dinosaurs. Larger dinosaurs that were not afraid of being attacked and eaten by other dinosaurs would probably have been more colourful.

The feathers may have been short and looked like hair, but, scientists have discovered that the skin covering was hollow (like a feather) instead of solid (like hair).

What's the difference between male and female dinosaurs?

This is still a mystery to scientists and we don't really know. It is thought that female dinosaurs mght have had wider hips because they laid eggs.

The difference between male and female dinosaurs would depend on the species.

Females might have been more brightly coloured, or males might have been more brightly coloured, which might have made it easier to tell the difference between male and female feathered dinosaurs.

In some dinosaur species the fully grown adult may have been a different size, so the female might have been bigger than the male, or vice versa.

In many dinosaur species it would have been difficult to tell the difference between males and females from their appearance.

Dinosaur Poo

Fossilised poo is called *coprolite*. The word comes from two Greek words: '*kopros*' which means 'dung' and '*lithos*' which means 'stone'.

Fossilised dinosaur poo has helped people learn a lot about dinosaurs. It can tell us about what different species of dinosaurs ate. Coprolite is often extremely valuable to scientists in their research to discover more about different dinosaur species. it can also be extremely valuable to collectors, who pay thousands of pounds for rare dinosaur coprolite.

The first fossilised dinosaur poo was discovered in the early 1800s by Mary Anning who lived near Lyme Regis on Britain's 'Jurassic Coast'. This part of Devon and Dorset is famous for the many fossils found from the Triassic, Jurassic and Cretaceous periods. Whilst excavating *ichthyosaur* and *plesiosaur* fossils she noticed some unusual cone-shaped rocks. At the time the objects were called 'bezoar stones'. A bezoar is a hard mass of things that an animal has swallowed, like seed or hair, that has got trapped in its stomach. Mary noticed that the stones contained fossilised fish bones and other animal bones, trapped in the rock like a bezoar would trap things in a stomach. Her theory was that she had discovered fossilised poo. She discussed her theory with a famous scientist, William Buckland, who agreed with her theory and invented the word coprolite.

Mary Anning

Mary Anning is one of the most important people in the history of dinosaur discovery. As a small child she used to comb the beach with her father and brother, looking for what they called 'curiosities'. As she was from a poor family, they would clean and sell the curiosities. This was before many people knew the word 'fossil'.

Mary was 12 when her father died, so she had to then search for fossils every day in order to earn money for her family. With her brother, Joseph, she found an *Ichthyosaurus* skull. When she returned to where the skull was found, she discovered the rest of the 5.2 metre long skeleton. The word '*Ichthyosaurus*' means 'fish lizard', which is not very accurate, as it is a reptile that lived in the sea. The fossil was sold for a lot of money and helped Mary's family's money problems.

In 1823, Mary also discovered the first complete *Plesiosaurus*. At first people thought it was a fake. The Geological Society had a meeting to discuss Mary's find, but Mary wasn't invited.

For the rest of her life, Mary discovered many fossils, which were bought by scientists who wrote about the finds. Usually, Mary's name was not mentioned and she wasn't given credit for her discovery.

Mary came from a poor background, and only had a limited education at school. She was able to read, borrowed books and studied paleantology. She was not allowed to join the Geological Society, attend lectures and meeting. When the family hit poor times in 1820, Thomas

Birch, a local naturalist sold some of his valuable fossils to raise money which he gave Mary. He had bought many of the fossils from Mary and he told people about the great contribution Mary had made to the study of dinosaurs.

However, 200 years later, she is recognised as one of the most important people in the history of fossils and the study of dinosaurs.

What sounds did dinosaurs make?

Films and video games have created sounds for dinosaurs. Are these sounds anything like the real sounds that dinosaurs would have actually made? Films have combined the sounds of a baby elephant, wolves, crocodile and tiger to make terrifying sounds to match the scene.

Some dinosaurs would have made noises without opening their mouths, which would have been a very low rumbling sound. This is common with birds and reptiles. Scientists have looked at similar animals to dinosaurs, such as crocodiles and birds - in particular, big birds like ostriches. They have also studied dinosaur fossils, in particular fossilised syrinxes (vocal organs - the part of the body that makes sounds).

Non-avian dinosaurs (dinosaurs not linked to birds) didn't have a vocal organ. They would have made sounds by pushing out air. Looking at dinosaur fossils, it is sometimes possible to discover what their nasal passages were like. So blowing air though the nasal passages might have created sounds like a brass instrument - such as horns, trumpets and trombones. Dinosaurs would have probably been able to hiss, like geese.

Dinosaurs would have made sounds from their physical size: their steps would have made the ground shake.

How fast could dinosaurs run?

Some dinosaurs were very slow-moving because they were big and heavy. Other dinosaurs were light and could run as fast as the fastest land animals today.

Scientists look at a dinosaur's body size and build, then measure the distances between footprints. The scientists then compare their observations with current animals.

So how fast was the fastest dinosaur? Well, we cannot be certain but it might have been the *Struthiomimus* which may have reached speeds of 60 mph.

Gallimimus, a dinosaur that has been described as copying chickens could probably run at a similar speed to an ostrich. The *Gallimimus* had a long neck, legs and tail, and a small head with a long beak.

Dinosaur Eggs

What came first - the dinosaur or the egg? Well, before you have a dinosaur, there is a dinosaur in an egg.

How big were dinosaur eggs? Obviously, small dinosaurs would have laid small eggs, but would huge dinosaurs have laid proportionally bigger eggs? Yes, huge dinosaurs would have laid bigger eggs but the maximum size would have been about 60 cm in diameter. The smallest non-avian (not bird-related) dinosaur egg fossil was discovered in Japan. It is only 4.5 cm long and 2 cm in diameter. The smallest avian dinosaur eggs would have been about 2.5 cm long. Most dinosaur eggs would have been about 30 cm in length - the size of a standard ruler.

Dinosaur eggs would have been more rounded and symmetrical than oval birds' eggs. Dinosaurs would have laid several eggs (a clutch of eggs) at a time. There could be 4- 5 eggs in the clutch or many eggs, like a turtle lays. Not all the eggs would hatch. Mother dinosaurs would usually protect their eggs from other dinosaurs, and keep them warm.

Why did dinosaurs become extinct?

Dinosaurs were 'wiped off the Earth' 3 times. Firstly, at the end of the Triassic Period, secondly, at the end of Jurassic Period and finally at the end of Cretaceous Period.

The end of the Triassic Period

Volcanic eruptions on a huge scale across the land mass of Pangaea warmed the atmosphere, creating global warming. The volcanos threw out gas and lava for about 40,000 years.

Gas from the volcanos turned the oceans acidic. About 3/4 of land and marine species were killed.

The end of the Jurassic Period

It is not known for certain, but there are 3 theories about the cause:

1   Volcanic activity on a huge scale across land and water for many years, covering land and seabeds with lava. The volcanos might have destroyed land and caused widespread flooding.

2   Climate change (which is a major worry facing people today). The Earth has had many ice ages and at other times, the Earth has been very hot. An ice age or a period where the Earth became very hot may have caused the end of the Jurassic Period.

3   A huge meteorite (a rock from outer space) could have crashed into the Earth, sending debris across the globe and shaking the planet with massive shock waves and throwing all living creatures around.

The end of the Cretaceous Period

The end of the Cretaceous Period also marked the end of the 'Age of the Dinosaurs' - the Mesozoic Era.

Sixty-six million years ago, dinosaurs became extinct. They had dominated the planet for over 140 million years. Humans have 'only' been around for two hundred thousand years.

There are a number of theories about why dinosaurs became extinct.

Main Theory explaining dinosaur extinction

An asteroid named Chicxulub hit the Earth. An asteroid is similar to a meteorite, but bigger: it can be as big as a planet. Chicxulub was about 6.2 miles (10 km) wide and struck the Earth at over 43,000 miles an hour, landing in the Yucatan peninsular, which is in southern Mexico. The force of the explosion was as powerful as 10 billion atomic bombs, and it formed a crater that was 12 miles deep and about 93 miles wide.

When Chicxulub hit the Earth, it sent soot into the sky, which blocked out the sun. Temperatures rose, plants died and plant-eating animals had nothing to eat. The plant-eating animals died and then the animals that ate the plant-eating animals died. In the end, Chicxulub killed off three-quarters of Earth's animals including most of the dinosaurs except those that evolved to become birds.

The Nadir Crater

There is a possibility that there was more than one asteroid that hit the Earth 66 million years ago. The Nadir Crater was caused by an asteroid hitting the

Earth, about 250 miles off the west coast of Africa, covered by 300 metres of sea in the Atlantic Ocean. It would have caused a huge tidal wave, called a tsunami, over a kilometre high. There would have been an earthquake caused by the asteroid hitting the Earth. However, it was much smaller than the Chicxulub asteroid.

Were dinosaurs dying out already before the asteroid?

Scientists believe that the number of dinosaurs was declining before asteroids hit the Earth. Sea levels had got higher and more land was covered by the sea so there was less land for dinosaurs to live on. Changes in the plants growing on Earth meant that plant-eating dinosaurs lost their source of food.

Volcanic super eruptions in a part of the Earth which is now in India may have also killed off dinosaurs. India's Deccan

Plateau is one of Earth's largest volcanic features. It covers much of southern India. Geologists studying the rock have discovered that it was made by volcanos.

An alternative theory to explain why dinosaurs finally died out

Breaking wind (farting) might be the reason behind dinosaur extinction. Scientists have calculated the amount of gas produced by sauropods, basing their sums on how much gas would be made if cows were the size of huge dinosaurs.

The gas produced is methane, which is called the 'greenhouse gas' because it traps heat so the planet heats up. The extinction of dinosaurs was at a time when the Earth was warming up and becoming very hot. Dinosaurs producing huge amounts of methane, leading to global warming, might be why dinosaurs could no longer live on Earth.

Of course, it could have been a number factors; volcanos, asteroids, dinosaur flatulence and so on...

The Bronosaurus rightly gets its name back

The *Brontosaurus* was re-named the *Apatosuarus*, because the *Apatosaurus* came first - it was thought that the *Brontosaurus* was actually an *Apatosaurus*. The mistake was made due to a mix-up with fossil heads. In 2015 after examining the necks of the two dinosaurs, it was confirmed that the the *Brontosaurus* and the *Apatosuarus* were different kinds of dinosaur. Their heads and spine are different.

Brontosaurus
name means 'thunder lizard'

Apatosaurus

Name means 'deceptive lizard'

Tyrannosaurus Rex

The *Tyrannosaurus Rex*, often shortened to the *T-Rex*, is one of the most popular dinosaurs featuring in many films.

Its powerful jaws and sharp teeth meant it had a bite three times the force of a great white shark: it could slice straight through the head of its prey. It had 60 teeth which were sharp and serrated. Its teeth were used to kill and chop up its prey before swallowing meat whole - it didn't chew.

It lived for about 28 years. When it was young, it could run pretty fast. When fully grown, it could run at 10 miles an hour, which is about the speed that humans can run.

It is thought that females were bigger than males.

The *Tyrannosaurus Rex* had short arms. They were about 90 cm long. If a tall man (about 1.8 metres tall) had arms in proportion to a T-Rex, his arms would only be 12.5 cm long. No-one knows why *Tyrannosaurus Rex* had such short arms.

Clearly, its arms are too short to help it eat. One theory is that they used their short arms to hold on to each other. It's strange to think of such fierce dinosaurs cuddling each other in a loving way! Perhaps the short arms were used to lift themselves off the ground if they had been sleeping or had fallen over. Another theory is that the short arms would be used to hold squirming prey. It is also possible they used their short arms to attack prey.

Tyrannosaurus Rex

Species Theopod

Era Late cretaceous

Name meaning 'King of the tyrant lizards'

Food meat-eater

Approximate size 12 metres long 3.5 metres high

Weight 5 -7 thousand kg

The *Tyrannosaurus Rex* is probably the most famous of all the dinosaurs, probably because it was fierce.

Tyrannosaurus Rex jaws

A young *T-Rex* jaw-power would have
been similar to a crocodile, 19 times more
powerful than a human. An adult would
have been well over a 116 times more
powerful than a human.

Iguanodon

In 1825 it became the second species recognised by scientists as a dinosaur. It had a long tail which helped it balance. It walked on all 4 limbs and ate low-growing plants. On 2 legs it might have been able to run at about 12-15 mph but it wasn't able to gallop on 4 legs.

It had spikes on its thumbs, which it probably used like a short bayonet to fight other dinosaurs. Possibly it might have been used to break up food such as fruit or seeds.

Iguanodon

Species Ornithopod

Era jurassic early cretaceous

Name meaning 'iguana-tooth'

Food plants

Approximate size 11 metres long 3.5 metres high

Weight 4 -5 thousand kg

The second dinosaur to be named, after an *Iguanodon* fossil was found in Sussex. Lived in herds, had 3 - toed feet similar to modern cows.

Corythosaurus

Species Ornithopod

Era late cretaceous

Name meaning 'helmet lizard'

Food plants

Approximate size 10 metres long 2 metres high

Weight 4 thousand kg

It had wide, webbed hands and feet, as it lived near water, it may have been able to swim. Its skin had small pebbly scales which were probably brightly coloured.

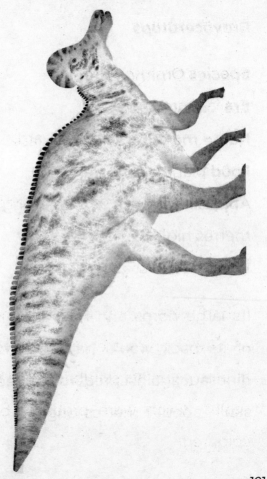

Bravoceratops

Species Ornithopod

Era cretaceous

Name meaning 'wild horn face'

Food plants

Approximate size 9 metres long 3 metres high

Weight 7 thousand kg

Its large horns and frills along the top of its back would have defended the dinosaur against predators. It had a huge skull - about 3 metres long.

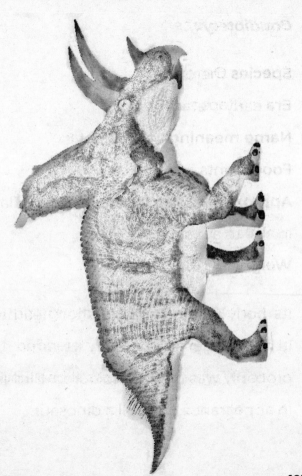

Caudipteryx

Species theropod

Era early cretaceous

Name meaning 'tail feather'

Food plants and insects

Approximate size 1 metre long -similar in size to a peacock

Weight 2 kg

Its body was covered in short feathers, it had longer feathers on its arms and probably was brightly coloured. Bird-like in appearance, but still a dinosaur.

Parasaurolophus

Species hadrosaurid (duck-billed)

Era late cretaceous

Name meaning 'beside crested lizard'

Food plants

Approximate size 10 metres long 3 metres high

Weight 5 thousand five hundred kg could run on 2 legs

Its mouth is similar in appearance to a ducks beak. Scientists believe that it would have been able to make loud honking sounds.

Kentrosaurus

Species Stegosaur

Era late jurassic

Name meaning 'spiked lizard'

Food plants

Approximate size 5 metres long 3 metres high

Weight 1 thousand kg

Running along the top of its back were two rows of bony plates, arranged in pairs. Its soft underbelly was vulnerable if attacked. Its head was close to the ground so it could easily eat vegetation.

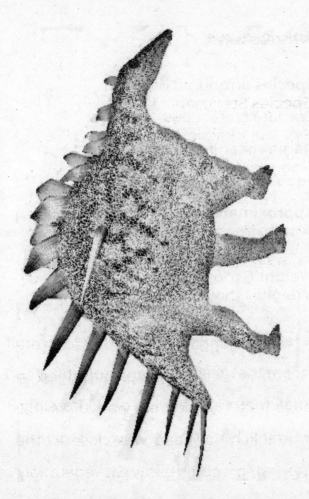

Ankylosaurus

Species armoured dinosaur

Era late cretaceous

Name meaning 'fused lizard'

Food plants

Approximate size 10 metres long 1.7 metres high

Weight 6 thousand kg

Scientists believe that its large throat meant that it also had large tongue, it had small teeth and a wide beak. Possibly it was pink, but nobody knows for certain.

Jokes

What do you call a sleeping dinosaur?

A dinosnore.

What do you get if you cross a dinosaur with a firework?

Dinomite.

Why did the dinosaur cross the road?

Because chickens hadn't evolved yet.

How do you offer a dinosaur a hot drink?

Tea, Rex?

What would you call a dinosaur who wears dark sunglasses?

A Doyouthink Hesaurus.

Why did the dinosaur cross the road?

To eat the chicken on the other side.

What do you call a dinosaur at a rodeo?

A Broncosaurus.

What do you call a dinosaur in a scary film?

A Terror Dactyl.

What's slimy, see-through and hangs from trees?

Dinosaur snot.

What should you do when a dinosaur sneezes?

Get out of the way as fast as you can.

What should you do if you see a meat-eating dinosaur?

Hide and make sure it doesn't see you.

What's just a big as a dinosaur, but doesn't weigh anything?

A dinosaur's shadow.

What always followed dinosaurs?

A dinosaur tail.

What do you call the tool dinosaurs use to cut wood?

A dino-saw.

What does a triceratops sit on?

A tricera bottom.

What do you call a dinosaur with one eye?

Eye-saur.

What do you call a group of dinosaurs singing together?

Tyranno-chorus?

What do you call a dinosaur ghost?

A scary-dactyl.

Which dinosaur could jump higher than a tree?

Every dinosaur. Trees can't jump.

What is in the middle of dinosaurs?

The letter S.

What do you call a dinosaur that hates losing?

A Saur-Loser.

What's the best way to lift a baby T. Rex?

With a crane.

What do you call a shop where dinosaurs go shopping?

A dino-store.

Why can't you hear a Pterodactyl having a wee?

Because the P is silent.

What do you get if you cross a dinosaur with explosives?
Dino-mite.

What do you call a dinosaur that talks all the time and never listens to what others have to say?
A dino-bore.

What do dinosaurs need to drive their cars?
Fossil fuels.

What happens when dinosaurs crash their cars?

You get T Wrecks.

What sort of dinosaur would Harry Potter be?

A dino-sorcerer.

What's the name of the dinosaur that had to wear glasses?

Tyrannosaurus Specs.

What was a dinosaur's favourite number?

8 - Ate.

What do you call a polite dinosaur?

A Pleasey thankyousaur.

What do you call a dinosaur with its eyes closed?

A doyouthink hesaraus.

What do dinosaurs put on their fish and chips?

Dinosauce.

What do call twin dinosaurs?

A Pair-odactlys.

What do you say when you meet a 2-headed dinosaur?

Hello, hello.

Why do museums and dinosaur parks have old dinosaur bones?

Because there aren't any new dinosaur bones.

What's the dinosaur's favourite playground toy?

A dino-seesaw.

What is a Triceratops' favourite musical instrument?

A horn.

Why did the dinosaur have a sticking plaster?
Because it had a din-sore. dino-sore?

Why shouldn't you let a dinosaur read you a story at bedtime?
Because its tales are too long.

What do you call a dinosaur that never takes a bath?
A stinkyosaurus.

Where does a dinosaur go sun-bathing?

At the Dino-shore.

What do you call a dinosaur with the runs?

A dino-sorearse.

What do you call a dinosaur fart?

A blast from the past.

How do meat-eating dinosaurs like their meat?

Rawrrrr.

Who started all the dinosaur jokes many years ago?

That's what dinosaurs would like to know!